750 HIGH SCORE
630 YOUR SCORE

ISBN 0 361 06344 X

Published 1984 by Purnell Books, Paulton, Bristol,
BS18 5LQ, a member of the BPCC Group.
Made and printed in Great Britain by Purnell and Sons
(Book Production) Limited, Paulton, Bristol.
Phototypeset by Quadraset Limited.

GERRY ANDERSON
& CHRISTOPHER BURR'S

TERRAHAWKS™

Storybook

CONTENTS

EXPECT the UNEXPECTED

The base on the planet Mars, set up by scientists from Earth in the year 2020, had long been empty of human life. There were only robots and scanning machines to see the approach of what, at first, looked like a bright star in the distant sky.

It grew larger and larger, until at last it became recognisable as six separate ships, in close formation. Alien ships. Their approach clearly menacing.

Without warning, the attack fleet from somewhere deep in the Alpha Centauri star system opened fire, and energy bolts smashed down to blow the Mars Expedition Station to fragments!

Silently, the six spacecraft drew closer together, and linked to form a complete network. Then, slowly, they came down on vertical landing jets to settle themselves into the Martian dust . . .

The invaders had been expected. Their journey had taken several years, even at the speed of light, and, on Earth, an elite fighting force had been organised to meet the attacks which were certain to come from the Red Planet. That force was known as—Terrahawks!

In the force headquarters, the White House, based somewhere in South America, Lieutenant Hiro sat beside Doctor Tiger Ninestein in Hawknest Control. Ninestein, chief of Terrahawks, was studying a satellite picture of the aliens' new base on Mars. "This looks like our first ten-thirty," he said, using the jargon that meant 'standby'.

"Exactry," said Hiro. Being Japanese, he was usually unable to pronounce his Ls properly.

Ninestein shot him an amused glance. "So you'd better get up to your station on Spacehawk, Hiro. Have a good *fright*."

The joke was lost on Hiro, who made his way to Treehawk, the shuttle vehicle that they used to go from headquarters to their 'watchdog' space station, far above Earth. Treehawk was concealed within a large specimen tree standing in the grounds of the White House, and as Hiro received a 'ten-fifty'—the order to go—the tree opened up like an upside-down umbrella, and Treehawk's photon engines roared into life.

With Hiro on his way, Ninestein went to the quarters of Kate Kestrel, his Captain in charge of the aircraft called Hawkwing. Kate, a talented musician and singer, was busy running over a new tune on her synthesiser, and Tiger Ninestein had to shout to get her attention.

"I take it that earthquake was Hiro lifting off," she grinned at him, and he nodded.

"The Martians," he began . . .

"Martians?" Kate frowned.

"Well, that's what they are now, Kate," said Ninestein. "The latest picture shows a part of their base breaking away from what appears to be their mother ship."

"An attack?" Kate raised her eyebrows.

"Could be. We're on our first ten-thirty."

Lieutenant Hiro arrived on Spacehawk to find Space Sergeant 101 waiting for him. 101 was one of the regiment of globe-shaped Zeroids that formed Terrahawks' main work-force. Hiro greeted him, but gave his first attention to the collection of house-plants that were his pride and joy. "I hope you've been talking to them while I was away, like I told you," he said, this time pronouncing his Ls quite well.

"Yes, sir," replied 101.

"You know something, 101? Doctor Ninestein's theory is that my plants flourish because of the artificial gravity up here, and when I explain it's because I talk to them—do you know what he says?"

"That you're a nut, sir?" said 101.

"Exactry!" beamed Hiro, and settled down in front of the screens to watch for any sign of danger.

Back on Earth, Ninestein was relaxing in the way he liked best—at a video game where he was always trying to improve on his score of shooting down spaceships. His second-in-command, Mary Falconer, watched with amusement, and so did Sergeant Major Zero, commander of the Zeroids.

"Seven hundred and forty-five points!" crowed Ninestein, jiggling the video-game control. "I'm going to top my best yet!" But just at

that moment, the picture on screen cut out, to be replaced by the anxious face of Hiro! Mary winced, Zero chuckled—but softly—and Tiger Ninestein looked as if he was ready to burst a blood vessel! "Confound it," he roared. "Of all the . . . "

Hiro interrupted. "I have a contact, Doctor. Trajectory, Mars to Earth."

Ninestein calmed down. Now his face was deadly serious as he turned to Mary. "I'm calling a ten-forty."

It meant Battle Stations, and as the alarm shrieked in Kate Kestrel's quarters, she grabbed her flying gear and let some Zeroids transport her towards the Hawkwing launch tunnel.

On Spacehawk, Zeriods 1 to 100 each went to their action positions, ready to open fire at a moment's notice, and Hiro stood by the video screen that showed him Ninestein's face. "Any visual sighting yet, Hiro?" said Ninestein.

Hiro shook his head, but turned to 101. "Anything, Sergeant?"

"I'll check again, sir," said the Zeroid.

Ninestein turned to Mary in Terrahawk control. "They *must* have a visual sighting by now," he muttered.

Mary shrugged. "The sensors have located a definite energy source, but one hundred Zeroids report nothing and one hundred Zeroids can't be wrong!"

"Neither can the sensors," said Ninestein. "We seem to have something invisible coming for us." Abruptly, he made up his mind. "Hiro. Lock on to that energy source—and blast it!"

"But, Doctor," said Hiro. "How do we know they're hostile? I mean, just because they're alien . . . "

"Don't argue with me, Hiro. Obey my orders and open fire!"

From their positions, the Zeroids on Spacehawk delivered a massive broadside, and a whole area of the sky seemed to light up with the power of enormous explosions. There was still nothing of the alien craft to be seen, but amazingly, the energy source kept on its course unharmed, and Space Sergeant 101 had to report, unbelievably, that it was through, and heading for Earth!

It was time for Hawkwing to take flight. Kate Kestrel sat at the controls of what they called 'The Egg'—complete with its own power unit. The rest of Hawkwing was devoted to the wing section, carrying high energy laser cannon and guided energy bolts, all under the command of her number two, Lieutenant Hawkeye. As Hawkwing's engines revved up to full power, a lake beyond the White House began to swirl, a vortex—a giant whirlpool—appearing in the centre of it. It was up through this vortex that Hawkwing emerged into the sunlight, flashing upwards towards the stratosphere!

"Airborne," said Kate.

Over her radio came Mary's voice. "Energy source approaching. Ionosphere at Mach six. It's a controlled descent."

"I have no radar echo," said Kate.

Now Ninestein broke in. "Kate, I'm going to pass co-ordinates to your on-board computer, then I want you to blast the whole area. You can't use guided missiles—there's nothing to lock on to."

"Ten-ten," said Kate. "Over to you, Hawkeye."

As the computer got Hawkwing into position, Hawkeye cut loose with the energy cannon . . . but still there was no result. Hawkeye said, grimly: "I fired at nothing—and guess what I hit!"

"Energy source has now entered Earth's atmosphere," reported Mary.

"What's the projected landing site?" asked Ninestein, and it was Sergeant Major Zero who replied.

"One hundred miles due north of Bangkok, sah. Might I suggest . . ."

"No you may not," snapped Ninestein. "Reason is not in your sphere."

"You don't think much of us, sah. I mean, as men. Do you?" Like all sergeant majors, Zero was fond of a good grumble.

But Ninestein spun round to shout at him. "For Pete's sake, Zero! Not now . . . !"

Zero rolled his way out and into the Zeroid barracks. Mary had told him to get a hundred Zeroids on board immediately, and he barked his orders. "All right, lads. Let's be having you. This is it."

The Terrahawk control lounge doubled as the flight deck of the huge transporter vehicle known as Battlehawk. With Mary at the instruments, Ninestein beside her, and Zero back on his perch, having seen his soldiers safely on board, the engines began to fire. Outside, the roof of the White House hinged open, the four walls folded outwards, and the Battlehawk roared upwards to clear the building. Behind it, the White House returned to its normal shape. Nobody would ever have suspected that such an innocent-looking area concealed such an enormous task-force!

Ninestein got in touch with Hawkwing. "Kate. Bring Hawkwing to the battle zone. We'll need air cover."

"We're on our way, Tiger," said the pilot.

Ninestein switched through to Hiro. "Move Spacehawk into geostationary orbit. I want you to keep an eye on the critical area."

"Ten-ten, Doctor," said Hiro.

Mary turned to the commander. "Well—this is going to be our first encounter with the new Martians, Tiger. What do you expect?"

"What do I expect?" His eyebrows lifted. "I—expect—the unexpected," he said after a moment's thought.

Battlehawk dropped Zeroids to take a closer look at the area where the invisible energy source had landed. They found nothing and, at last, Ninestein gave the order for Mary to take the huge craft down, ten miles away. Once the engines had died, Zero left to join his men, and Mary, choosing a nearby hill as a good vantage point, detached Terrahawk from the Battlehawk and flew it to the summit. There, she and Tiger waited for Zero's report.

"Tiger," said Mary, unable to stand his gloomy silence, "how does it feel to be one of nine clones?" For Ninestein was a very special sort of being. Like a cat, he had literally nine lives, and though it would be troublesome, there was always the means of re-creating him, should anything fatal happen to him.

He shrugged. "I suppose I feel the same as Zero feels. I mean—*he's* one of several hundred."

"You don't like him, do you?" said Mary.

"Zero? He's a robot, Mary. I don't think of him as a him. I think of him as an it!"

"Well, I think he's developed feelings, Tiger. It's possible, you know."

"Perhaps it is," said Ninestein gruffly. "Anyway—what the devil's he playing at? He's taking his time . . . "

At that moment, Zero's voice came through. "We've located the energy source, sah. I can't see it, but I sense its presence." He paused. "It seems to be under the bough of a tree, sah."

"You have to be joking, Zero," said Ninestein warningly. But Zero insisted he was right.

"Very well," said Ninestein. "Give it a burst of fire—and then beat it."

"Beat it? You mean—*retreat*?" The Sergeant Major hated even using that word!

"Just open fire, will you?"

The bough of the tree in question blew to bits.

Zero said: "The energy source is still there, but it's moved to one side."

"Use macrovision," said Ninestein impatiently.

The Sergeant Major focused on the ground about ten feet away. Suddenly, he shouted: "Stone me! I see a spaceship! *Under a gigantic spider!*"

Could it be true? Mary looked nervously at Ninestein, but he shook his head. "Macrovision, Mary. The spider's not gigantic. It's the spaceship that's minute. That's why we've never been able to see it or get a radar trace."

"We're getting one now," said Mary grimly. "That ship's grown! It's able to change its mass! Whoever's inside is able to control matter!"

Although Ninestein yelled for Zero to withdraw, the Sergeant Major chose to ignore the order. "Right, you lot. You know what they say. The bigger they are, the harder they fall! Take up defensive positions!"

All at once, a voice boomed out over the spaceship's address system. It was an evil, cackling voice. Like that of a witch!

"Can you hear me, earthman . . . ?"

For a moment, Zero glowed with pleasure. "Earth*man*! You mean *me* . . . ?"

The voice continued. "I believe that thirteen is an unlucky number

for some people here on earth . . ." There was a sound like the crack of a whip, and a bolt of energy from the alien craft hit Zeroid 13, and vaporised it instantly!

"Men! Open fire!" yelled Zero, leaping for cover.

It began to look desperate. The Zeroids were taking casualties from the alien's 'whipflash' weapons, while their own bolts were exploding harmlessly short of the enemy.

"Hawkwing!" rapped Ninestein. "That ship's got a force-field around it. We need your help."

"Ten-ten," said Kate Kestrel. "Get the Zeroids out of there. There's going to be a big bang!"

Hawkeye detached his gun-pod from Hawkwing and joined Kate in the Egg. They were going to use the whole of Hawkwing as a missile to ram the alien. To put all their force into one massive blow!

Zero ignored Ninestein's orders once more and, though he withdrew his men to a safe distance, he kept firing at the enemy to keep them occupied while Kate began her dive.

"Don't leave it too late, Kate," warned Ninestein.

"It's never too late, Tiger," grinned the ace pilot, releasing Hawkwing at the very last moment!

The mighty aircraft smashed into the alien as the Egg climbed clear, and there was a gigantic explosion as both craft blew to pieces!

"Fantastic, Kate! Just fantastic!" yelled Ninestein. "But you left the breakaway dangerously late!"

"That had to be the most exciting moment of my life!" grinned Kate. "And I don't take chances. My reflexes are faster than yours. Remember, I'm younger."

"True, but I'm wiser," said Ninestein, grinning.

"I was scared sick," said Hawkeye. "But then, I was never a good passenger."

Abruptly, Ninestein turned to his control screen as a blipping sound filled Terrahawk. When he spoke, his voice was shaking with disbelief. "The energy source is still there! It's re-building!"

It was true. And more than that, the alien ship had re-appeared right beside them on the hill, dwarfing Terrahawk!

Ninestein just had time to tell Mary to keep calm, before there was a burst of energy that surrounded him, and he vanished! White-faced, Mary could only stare at his empty seat, as if hypnotised . . .

The Doctor was unharmed. Somehow, he kept calm, even though, in the twinkling of an eye, he found that he had been transported aboard

the alien ship. He was facing a witch-like figure with a truly hideous appearance. It was Zelda, queen of the planet Guk. The fantastic mind behind the take-over of Mars and, now, the assault on Earth. "You should have known better than to attack us, Doctor," she crooned.

"But—but *we* did not attack," faltered Ninestein.

"Silence!" screamed Zelda. "How dare you speak to me like that! You—a mere human being!"

Ninestein remained cool. "*You're* not human?"

Zelda cackled. "My people were once the slaves of humans on our planet. We were their robots. But soon, our intelligence was greater than that of our creators, and we destroyed them. But enough of this talk! You are coming back with us to Mars!"

"You'll have to pass Spacehawk," said Ninestein. "It'll blast you out of the sky. My guess is that you have too little power left to reduce your ship's size, or keep up your force-field."

"Correct," admitted Zelda. "But they won't fire with *you* aboard."

Ninestein smiled. "You've slipped up, android. I'm only one of nine clones. If I die, there'll be another Ninestein within twenty-four hours."

On Spacehawk, Hiro was monitoring Ninestein's voice. The lieutenant looked nervous, but he knew his duty. Even as the alien ship

rose within range, he gave the order, and the massed Zeroids on the space-station delivered a broadside that utterly shattered Zelda's ship!

Yet, even as it exploded into a million pieces, Mary Falconer jerked out of her trance to see Tiger Ninestein sitting beside her—intact and unhurt!

"Tiger! Thank heavens! But—but how . . . ?"

"Well done, Hiro," said Ninestein into the communicator. Then: "I had a theory, Mary. Rather complicated. But I figured that if their ship was destroyed, their power to hold me would also be destroyed."

"And you were right," breathed Mary, wide-eyed.

"Yes. I'm glad to say." He turned again to the communicator. "Zero. We are rejoining Battlehawk. I want you back on board."

Terrahawks returned to stand-by duty at base. And it was there that Ninestein sent for Sergeant Major Zero.

"Today," he said, "you disobeyed orders. You started to think for yourself. Well, I've got news for you. You're a *machine*. You'll behave like one, do you hear me?"

"But, Doctor . . . " began Zero unhappily . . .

"Don't Doctor me," bellowed Ninestein. "In future, when I say jump—you *jump*!"

Mary and Kate interrupted. They were looking stonily at their commander.

"I happen to believe that Sergeant Major Zero behaved like a real man today, Tiger," said Mary.

"That's right," agreed Kate. "If he hadn't drawn the enemy fire, Hawkeye and I might not have been here tonight for the party."

"Party?" frowned Ninestein.

"Yes. In the White House. To celebrate the defeat of the invaders," said Kate. "Come on."

Ninestein shook his head wearily and followed the girls. While Zero bounced up and down with delight. "Like a man! She said I behaved like a *man*!" he kept saying, over and over again!

The party was going well, when an interruption came from Spacehawk. It was Hiro, and the news grave.

"Zelda's on her way back."

"That's impossible," spluttered Ninestein. But then, Zelda's own voice came through, loud and clear.

"Nothing in this universe is impossible, Doctor. When my ship lost its power to control matter, you were automatically returned to Earth. And *I* to Mars. But fear not. For despite your hostility, I return to Earth—in peace!"

"Peace?" said Ninestein, his voice cracking. "I don't believe it! Terrahawks—Battle stations! I'm calling a ten-forty!"

Zelda's ship came to a halt beyond the range of Spacehawk's weaponry. She said: "Earthmen, I come on a goodwill mission. I bring a gift from my people. I request safe conduct to your base so that I may confer with your commander."

"Our base is concealed," said Hiro. "Its position is revealed to no-one."

"Of course," replied Zelda soothingly. "Then let the meeting take place as before. I promise you—no tricks." Then, closing down her communicator so that they could hear nothing more of her voice, she added: "Gifts, yes. I have lots of little presents for our earthling friends!" She turned to where a stack of cube-like objects lay in formation behind her, and cackled with evil glee . . .

Battlehawk had taken off again, and had returned to the hill in the jungle, north of Bangkok. Hawkwing overflew the zone in wide circles, ready for anything. Hawkeye once more shifted his gun-bay to the Egg, joining Kate Kestrel. The flying section—Hawkwing itself—had been replaced in no time at all, and now they were ready to use it again, just as before.

"Zelda's about thirty miles south," Hawkeye told Ninestein. "She'll be landing in a few minutes."

"Ten-ten," said Ninestein. "Watch out for her, Mary."

Soon enough, the alien craft touched down nearby. And Zelda's voice came over the radio.

"Well, Doctor, you gave me safe pasage. Does that mean I have won your confidence?"

"No," said Ninestein shortly. "But for the moment, we are prepared to give the benefit of the doubt."

"You are very wise," crooned Zelda. "As you know, I have the power to control matter. I will now perform a small miracle for you. Look to the west, where the land is bright . . . "

There was an immense build-up of power from the alien ship. The sky seemed to darken, and bolts of energy flared among the hills. Alarmed, Ninestein barked orders. "Kate! Hawkeye! Attack! I don't know what's going on—but *ram* that ship!"

"Ten-ten," yelled Kate Kestrel. "Hang on to your hat, Hawkeye!" Once more, she threw Hawkwing into a steep dive, closing rapidly on the target.

But, at the last moment, Ninestein's voice came over again! "Pull out! Cancel attack!"

In the nick of time, Hawkwing climbed away, because, far from causing destruction, the power from Zelda's ship had created a vast and shining motorway where there had once been jungle! It reached away over the hills and into the distance!

"You have received your first gift," came Zelda's voice. "Think what other benefits I could bring to your planet. And now I shall leave—*if* you grant me safe conduct . . .?"

Baffled, Ninestein replied: "Y-yes. You have my word. Maybe you *do* want peace . . ."

Zelda took off and, obeying orders, Hiro on Spacehawk did nothing to prevent her return to Mars.

Meanwhile, Tiger Ninestein sat thoughtfully looking at the incredible new highway. At last, he said: "We'll take a closer look at it. It's about time I gave my old Roller a little air."

"Do you mean me, sah?" asked Zero brightly.

"No, Zero," snapped Ninestein. "My *Roller*. My Rolls-Royce. Just stay put, will you?"

The cargo-door of the Battlehawk was lowered, and a sleek vehicle purred into view. It was a magnificent vintage Rolls-Royce, restored to all its glory in Tiger Ninestein's workshops, and equipped with a computer which allowed it to think for itself, and even speak. It was called Hudson—standing for Heuristic Universal Driver with Sensory

and Orbital Navigation. "That is what I *call* a car," said Ninestein proudly. "It may be something similar to Zero, but this one has breeding!"

He blushed, as Hudson said: "I presume that rather coarse whistle of yours meant that my services were required?"

"Well—er—yes. Er—I thought we'd take a little ride down the new motorway, Hudson."

"Certainly, sir," replied the car. "Your voice-print is checked, and the doors are now unlocked. Welcome aboard, sir."

Ninestein and Mary got in. She was *very* impressed. "Electronics by Hiro, I presume?" she said. And Ninestein grinned.

"Exactry," he mimicked the lieutenant's voice.

"It's beautiful," said Mary admiringly. And Hudson coughed.

"I am too modest to imagine you meant me, madam," said the car. "But if you are referring to the highway, then *that* is undoubtedly of superlative quality. The surface is smooth, but with good traction. Very advanced engineering, in my opinion."

Something caught Tiger Ninestein's eye. "Pull up, Hudson, please," he said.

On both sides of the road there were scattered Cubes. Though featureless, they reminded Ninestein of giant dice.

"What are they?" said Mary.

"I don't know," replied Ninestein. "But they look—er—rather dicey to me. I think we ought to get out of here." His suspicions of Zelda had returned, and he was right!

Even as the Rolls-Royce began to move forwards, the groups of Cubes leapt into life. Some of them formed two posts, one on either side of the highway, and, between them, the amber glare of a force-field began to show!

"Reverse, Hudson," barked Ninestein. But it was too late! More of the Cubes had made themselves into posts behind the car, and now the force-field crackled to surround the vehicle on all sides!

"Trapped!" Ninestein banged his fist on the dashboard. "What a *fool* I was! Try the laser, Hudson . . . "

The Silver Lady mascot on the Rolls-Royce's bonnet swivelled, and a lance of energy shot from it. It had no effect at all on the force-field.

"Link me with Hiro, Hudson," said Ninestein wearily.

"Calling all Terrahawks," said Ninestein. "This is a mayday. A ten-ninety. We are trapped in what I think is an impenetrable force-field. Stand by for instructions but, in the meantime, make no attempt to rescue us."

Zelda's shrill voice came back to him from space. "I promise that *I* will not try to rescue you, Doctor," she cackled. "You will remain there until you both die! I bid you farewell, while I go to make new plans for the taking over of your foolish planet!"

Hawkeye broke in. "Kate and I reckon we can drop supplies to you through the top of the force-field, sir," he said. But at that very moment, the amber-coloured crackling made a sort of roof over the posts, and Hudson and his occupants were completely sealed off!

"Tiger," said Mary. "I hate to say this, but Zero is the only one who can save us."

Ninestein scowled. "The thinking man's thinking robot? Hang it, I believe you're right. He can increase his mass. Without growing in size, he can make himself almost as heavy as a black hole in space! If he hit one of these posts he could break the field."

"But we can't call him," said Mary helplessly. "All communication has gone."

It was lucky indeed that Sergeant Major Zero *had* learned to think for himself. "*He* don't deserve it," he muttered as he bounced off his perch in the Battlehawk, "but I can't leave Mary to rot. Not no way, not no-*how*!"

Zero got himself into position, and began to increase his mass. There was nothing special to be seen about him, but his power was so great that, as he began to roll down the hill, two big trees in his path were snapped off like matchsticks! Way above him, Kate and Hawkeye watched from Hawkwing, yelling encouragement! "Go, Zero! Go, go, GO!"

Zero's incredible weight was making deep tracks in the ground by the time his lumbering shape hit one of the force-field's corner posts. And the result was truly spectacular! There came an incredible blast of released power, and the crackling amber sheets of light disintegrated!

Hudson rolled down his passenger window, and Mary looked out, wiping her brow. "Sergeant Major," she whispered, "you were magnificent!"

Zero, his mass returned to normal, bounced coyly. "It was nothing, ma'am. Nothing at all."

"You're right," said Ninestein, half to himself, but Mary rounded on him angrily.

"Tiger!" she said.

"All right, all right! Just my little joke," he said, raising his hands defensively.

Much later, Terrahawks re-grouped in the White House. It was time they resumed their interrupted party, and this time they knew that they really had beaten Zelda in the first round of the battle of wits.

Tiger Ninestein looked sternly at Sergeant Major Zero. "You've been consistently disobeying orders, Zero," he said grimly. "Thinking for yourself against all orders. I've only got one thing to say to you."

The others got ready to start protesting on the Sergeant Major's behalf, but then Ninestein's face broke into a smile, and he patted his commanding Zeroid on the dome. "Yes," he repeated. "Just one thing to say. And that's 'thanks'. Now come and join the party . . . "

Whooping with delight, Sergeant Major Zero bounced after the boss and his officers. He'd been called a hero, a man, and now even Tiger Ninestein had given him a kind word. Not even the thought of Zelda could dampen his spirits!

THE MIDAS TOUCH

It was to be a very special occasion in Hawknest. Tiger Ninestein's birthday party, to be exact. Presents had been bought, a cake had been baked, and Kate Kestrel had written and rehearsed a new song in Ninestein's honour. Up on Spacehawk, Lieutenant Hiro boarded Treehawk to come down to Earth for the celebration, leaving Space Sergeant 101 in charge of the Terrahawks' powerful satellite.

But there was trouble on the horizon. In permanent orbit above the world lay a large cargo spaceship called 'Space Fort Knox'. It was unmanned, but the inside, heavily protected by laser beams, held an enormous amount of gold bullion in glittering bars. Worst of all, the evil Zelda had found out about it!

In her Martian base, Zelda chuckled nastily as she faced her beastly sister, Cystar, and her even uglier son, Yungstar. "We shall attack and destroy this carrier of gold," she said. "And then the earthlings' greed will ensure their own extinction!"

"How will we do it, mother?" asked Yungstar brightly.

"With a little help—from the Krell!" cackled Zelda. "Come! Launch the ship, and we shall put it to the test!"

Zelda's craft flew over the Martian surface at a low angle, and a target rock, weighing several tons, was shot from the rear of it to land with a mighty crash in the flat, orange sand of the planet's main desert. Almost at once, not far away, there was a disturbance in the dirt, and a fearsome monster, almost covered by matted black hair, pushed its way out of hiding. This was the Krell, and its waving trunk swung this way and that, as if sniffing for prey!

Now it pointed directly at the target rock, and a terrific bolt of energy shot from the trunk to strike the massive rock and blow it to fragments!

Zelda screeched with triumph. "Magnificent," she yelled. "Just wait until the Krell destroys their precious gold-ship! The earthlings will panic. Their civilisation, built on such tokens of greed, will collapse! They will be at our mercy!"

On Earth, Kate Kestrel had finished her song for Tiger, and, pleased, the Terrahawks' leader took the glass of wine that Hiro offered him. The label read: 'Ninesteiner 1999'.

"This is tremendous, Hiro," said Ninestein. "Straight from the Terrahawk vineyard, no doubt."

"Of course, Doctor," replied Hiro. "And like you it has matured with age."

"Very dry," commented Sergeant Major Zero.

"Oh no. Quite sweet, in fact," said Hiro innocently, and everyone laughed.

Hawkeye gave Ninestein a book, 'Robots can be fun'. "That's food for thought," grinned Ninestein, glancing at Sergeant Major Zero. "Thank you!"

"Speaking of food," put in Mary Falconer. "Are you ready, Sergeant Major?"

Zero had been joined by one of his Zeroids—Number 18, the one with the French accent. Zero, showing off his knowledge of the language, said: "Ready, Dix-huit?"

The pair of them extended trumpet-shaped 'probes' from their round bodies and blew an electronic fanfare as Mary Falconer produced the cake. She had baked it in the shape of a Zeroid and, once again, everyone laughed.

Just then, a report came through from Spacehawk, where Space Sergeant 101 was still keeping watch. "I'm tracking a small craft from Mars," he said. "It's one of Zelda's Zeafs."

Tiger Ninestein sighed. "Better get back to Spacehawk, Hiro. Meanwhile, 101 is going to have to handle the situation. Come on, Mary—to Terrahawk."

Sergeant Major Zero watched the party break up. Then he contacted 101 direct. "This is our big chance to show 'em, lad. A Zeroid in command with no humans around to take the credit. Shoot that Zeaf down—but wait until you see the whites of their eyes, boy!"

"If you say so, Zero. But I hope you know what you're doing," replied 101. At his controls, 101 gave instructions to the Zeroids defending the space station. "Lock on to target—but hold your fire . . . "

Unfortunately, waiting was the wrong thing to do. Inside the Zeaf, the Krell fired first, and a bolt of energy hit Spacehawk squarely in the communications section!

In Terrahawk, Mary looked anxiously at Ninestein. "We've lost contact with Spacehawk. For some reason they didn't open fire!" On his perch, Sergeant Major Zero gulped and flapped his lids, looking guilty.

"Launch Hawkwing," snapped Ninestein.

Within moments, the sleek craft, with Kate Kestrel and Hawkeye, rose from the whirlpool above its launch tunnel and sped skywards. Already, the Zeaf had entered Earth's atmosphere, and Mary Falconer was computing the spot at which it would land. Over the radio, she told Kate: "Egypt! Right by the pyramids!"

When Hawkwing reached the area, Kate could see it there. Silent and ominous. Standing on the sand. "Sensors indicate a life-form," she said. "And my guess is that it hasn't come to make sandcastles!"

Ninestein looked baffled. "The Egyptian desert! What else is there, except sand? What's Zelda's target?"

"The pyramids?" suggested Mary, but Ninestein shook his head.

"Of great historic interest, but hardly of vital importance to Zelda. It could be Cairo, I suppose." He paused. "We'd better get out there, Mary. Stand by for lift-off."

The White House opened up and Battlehawk, carrying Ninestein, Mary and Sergeant Major Zero, lifted off through the gap, setting course eastwards. There was no way any of them could guess at Zelda's real plans!

On Mars, Yungstar was thinking about sand, too. He smacked his lips. "Fine-grained! Sun-scorched! Absolutely perfect if cooked with a little tar and served cold!"

"Be quiet, you drooling half-wit," snarled Zelda. "Little do those fools realise that, every four hours, the earthlings' treasure-ship passes directly over the very spot where the Krell now lurks! This time, not even Terrahawks can beat me!" Her shrill laughter filled the Martian base . . .

Hiro—now back on Spacehawk to supervise repairs to the communications centre—quizzed 101 about not firing in time. 101 didn't want to put the blame on Zero with his 'whites of the eyes' instruction, and muttered his apologies. "We'll put the damage right within one hour, lieutenant," said 101, changing the subject.

In the meantime, Kate Kestrel had overflown the Zeaf several times in Hawkwing. Now she gave Hawkeye the command to destroy it. "Let's blast that thing right back to Mars!"

Hawkeye, the team's master gunner, gave the Zeaf the full power of a burst of rapid cannon-fire, and he grinned as the alien ship blew up with a massive explosion. Kate reported to Ninestein, as Battlehawk approached, "Whatever was in that ship, we kicked a little sand in its face!"

"Ten-ten, Kate," said Ninestein. "Take us down, Mary. I want that wreckage searched. Get moving, Zero."

Manned by Megazoids, the Battletank dropped from Battlehawk and, as it rolled towards the point where the Zeaf had been, Zero and Zeroid 18 dropped down to follow, rolling across the sand. Nothing was moving.

"See anything, Dix-huit?"

"Oui. Sand."

"Watch it, lad,"grunted Zero.

"Of course I watch eet," said 18. "What else can I do?"

In that instant, something moved beneath the surface. It was the Krell, and its fearsome trunk-like snout turned towards the Battletank! "Stone me! Take cover, Dix-huit!" yelled Zero.

A near miss from the Krell rocked the Battletank. Then another. "Get out of there, Zero!" came Ninestein's barked command.

Zero shook his shutters defiantly, and stayed where he was. But now Ninestein was worrying about the Battletank. "It's outgunned," he snapped. "Pull it back, Mary!"

At that moment, Hiro's voice came over the communicator. "We're fully operational again, sir," he said.

Ninestein said: "Great. We may need you on this one!"

The Battletank had withdrawn, but Zero and 18 were still in the shelter of some rocks. "We were told to get clear," said 18.

"I'm staying, Dix-huit," said Zero. "It was—er—very nearly my fault that Spacehawk got hit. I want to try to make amends." He added: "No need for you to stay, of course."

"As zey say, in for a centime, in for ten francs," said 18.

"Well done. Brave lad," chuckled Zero.

Mary and Ninestein watched the Krell. "It was able to survive Hawkwing's attack," she said. "What are we up against, Tiger?"

"Something that's virtually indestructible, Mary," he replied.

Then another message came through from Hiro. "The Space Fort Knox satellite is about to pass over the alien's ground position, Doctor!"

"Flaming thunderbolts!" exclaimed Ninestein. "So that's the target! Eighty-five per cent of the world's gold reserves!"

The Krell's trunk was pointing upwards, at the sky. Almost too fast for the eye to see, a lancing shaft of power came from it—and way above the Earth, a crashing explosion shook the gold-ship!

"We've got to stop it! But how?" Mary's face was a deathly white.

"Only Spacehawk has the fire-power to take that thing out," said Ninestein. "Hiro—can you do it?"

Hiro was anxious. "We can concentrate enough energy, but at this range we could miss by a mile. We need a spotter on the ground to direct our fire . . . "

Sergeant Major Zero had heard. "Sah. I'm your man!"

"Zero!" roared Ninestein. "I thought I told you to pull back! Where are you?"

"Right near the monster, sah. And ready to do the spotting."

Mary said: "He could be killed, Tiger."

And Ninestein replied: "Yeah. He's very close. The odds aren't good." But then he came to a decision. "All right, Zero. You've got the job."

Space Fort Knox was being mercilessly pounded by the Krell's power. At any second, a direct hit could arrive—and that would mean utter destruction. On Spacehawk, Hiro forced himself to give his orders calmly. "Concentrate our fire into as small an area as possible, 101," he said.

The spacecraft's Zeroids banked together and let loose a bolt of energy that struck earth beyond the Krell and bounced Zero and Number 18 among the rocks!

"Left, left, sixty yards," said Zero shakily.

"Ten-ten," came 101's voice, and another blast of power tore into the desert almost on top of the Sergeant Major and his companion.

"Sacre bleu!" yelled 18.

"Quite," said Zero. "Bit too far over, 101. Right, right, thirty yards."

Then the Krell's deadly trunk swivelled round to point directly at the rocks that sheltered spotter and spotter's mate! "Stone me. I think the great hairy creep's spotted us, Dix-huit. We're for it now!"

"C'est la guerre," said 18.

The Krell took careful aim. Very careful aim. Helplessly, Zero muttered "Come on, Spacehawk . . . "

It was touch and go. In the split-second before the Krell was able to fire, the third blast of energy from Hiro's craft hurtled down and blew the monster to pieces! More than that, the stunning blast half-buried Sergeant Major Zero in a cascade of rocky debris!

He groaned. "To—to die in the line of duty! Killed on active service! Bury me here, Dix-huit—with full military honours!"

Number 18 extended a probe and ran it over Zero's body. "Pouf! Zere is nothing wrong with you! You are fine!"

"Oh," said Zero, a bit peeved. He had rather liked the idea of acting a death-scene, with his faithful Zeroids gathered round him in sorrow!

Way above the Earth, no more battered, luckily, than Zero himself, Space Fort Knox continued its orbit. And on Mars, Zelda took her rage out, as usual, on Cystar and Yungstar. She angrily struck a plate of cobalt-ore toast from her son's trembling hand . . .

Back at Hawknest, Zero was hovering about in the reception area of the White House. He was holding a long-range but snappish

conversation with Space Sergeant 101, up on Spacehawk.

"You little snitch, 101," muttered Zero. "I'll get even with you. You horrible . . . you . . . "

"I said nothing to anyone," came 101's voice, offended.

"Then why does Doctor Ninestein want to see me urgently?" said Zero.

At that moment, Ninestein yelled: "Zero!" The Sergeant Major bounced nervously into the Terrahawk Lounge.

"Sah. Before you start, sah. By 'whites of their eyes', I didn't mean . . . that is to say . . . it was all the Space Sergeant's fault! He's a right thick head . . . "

"What *are* you talking about, Zero?" interrupted Ninestein, baffled.

A moment's silence, and then, gulping, Zero went on. "Er. Nothing, sah. You wanted to see me, sah."

"You disobeyed a direct order to pull back."

"But I saved the situation, sah."

"That's not the point," growled Ninestein. "Have you anything to say?"

Mary grinned as Zero, thinking quickly, replied: "Yes, sah. Er—happy birthday."

Ninestein spread his hands and looked at the ceiling helplessly. Laughing, Mary produced the cake, on top of which she'd planted a single candle. "Yes, Tiger," she shouted. "Happy birthday!"

Without a word, Ninestein stooped and blew the candle out, but there was a twinkle in his eye as he did it . . .

GUNFIGHT at OAKY'S CORRAL

In the sun-scorched American desert, Sergeant Major Zero jumped up and showed himself for an instant above some rocks. Instantly, a blast of fire whipped the sun-helmet from his head and sent it spinning! "Stroll on! That was close," he muttered. "I've found 'em, sah," he added.

From Terrahawk, which had detached from Battlehawk to perch on a nearby hilltop, Doctor Tiger Ninestein said: "How many are there, Zero?"

"I'm showing meself, to draw their fire, sah," replied Zero. "Tell you in a moment." He bounced up again, and more shots zipped around him. He changed his position and tried a third time. At last he was satisfied. "Six of 'em, sah. Send in the Battlehawk, and let's give it 'em, in capital letters!"

The six in question were Zelda's Cubes. Her destructive alien 'soldiers'. A small party she had been able to land on Earth. And it was up to Terrahawks to destroy them!

Ninestein gave permission for the Battletank to be used, and Zero himself guided the craft to its target. "Roll out," he said, with relish. "Let 'em have it, my trusty Megazoids!"

Unfortunately, the Battletank's course was through the very gully where Sergeant Major Zero was positioned and, before he could get out of the way, it rolled over him and buried him in the dirt! It took him quite a long time to force himself out again, and he was only just in time to see the battle in which his Megazoids blew the Cubes to bits and gained the victory!

"They can dish it out but they can't take it, sah," he reported, bouncing the dust off himself. "Enemy destroyed."

"All right," said Ninestein. "Let's get back to Hawknest. Zero—I want the remains of those Cubes collected for examination . . . "

Some miles away, on the edge of the desert, there was a lonely cabin. A man named Sam Oaky lived there, and, frowning, he was on the telephone, having just dialled the number of Sheriff Cy Bull, chief of police in Badwater County. "Sure as heck there's a storm *somewhere*," muttered Sam Oaky. "Ah. That you, Sheriff . . . ?"

In his office, Cy Bull sprawled fatly in his chair, a sheen of sweat on his plump face. "Yup," he said. "Speak to me."

"This here's Sam Oaky, Sheriff."

"So?"

"You have a storm over your side?"

The chair groaned as the sheriff stood up and peered out of the window. He sat down again. "Nope. Last rain was last winter. You playin' me jokes, Sam?"

Oaky shook his head. "Could've sworn I heard thunder. Maybe I'll go out in the desert and take a look."

"Yeah, you do that, Sam," chuckled the sheriff. "Let me know if you find a snowball."

In the reception area of the White House, Sergeant Major Zero was boasting to one of his Zeroids—Number 21. "There I was," he said, "under constant fire, the sun beating relentlessly down, my helmet blown to pieces. I knew the moment had come to give the order."

"But-b-but," said 21 (who stammered), "I th-thought that Doctor N-N-N-Ninestein was in command!"

"Well he was, in a manner of speakin', lad. But I was the man on the ground. And that's where it counts."

"I thought you said you w-w-were *in* the g-g-ground, Sergeant M-M-Major . . . " stuttered 21.

Zero winced as he remembered how he was run over by the Battletank. "Well, I was. Er—dug in . . . "

"*Zero!*" The shout came from Ninestein himself. "Zero! Where the blazes are you?"

"He s-s-sounds angry," whispered 21. "I'd b-b-better be going!"

"He *do* sound a little irate," admitted Zero, bouncing away and cannoning into Ninestein's legs. "Ooops! Sorry, sah!"

"Just hold it, Zero," snapped Ninestein. "Where's the fire?"

"The only fire I see, sah, is the fire in your eyes," said Zero, but Ninestein ignored the remark.

"We have a problem. You reported six Cubes out in the desert. Hawkeye's been working on the pieces you collected, and we can account for only five. One Cube is missing."

"*Missing*, sah?"

"Missing, Sergeant Major," said Ninestein. "We're going back. I want that Cube located."

Ninestein, Mary Falconer and Zero positioned themselves in Battlehawk and, as the White House slid open, the massive craft made

its lift-off. It swung to horizontal flight, and set course towards the desert . . .

In his shack, Sam Oaky was on the telephone again. And once more, he was speaking to Sheriff Cy Bull. "I found it lying near a rock, Sheriff," he said. "Well, I tell you, it's the darndest thing I've ever seen." Sam glanced at a table nearby, upon which lay a Cube. One of Zelda's Cubes. One side of it was damaged, and it lay inert.

"Maybe I'll drive out tomorrow and take a look," said the sheriff. "'Bye now, Sam."

Oaky put down the phone and stared at the Cube. He wondered what on earth it could be . . .

Meanwhile, on Mars, Zelda was not in the best of moods. She frowned and muttered as she paced about, and Cystar glanced across at her nervously. "Is anything wrong, Zelda?" she said.

"For a moment, I thought one of the Cubes . . . No. It's nothing," said Zelda. She turned to glare at Yungstar, her son, who was licking his lips and rubbing his hands beside the dinner table.

"Oooh," he gurgled. "What a feast! Sandstone jelly! Feldspar soup! Granite crunchies with a sugaring of quicklime . . . "

"Stop jabbering!" snapped Zelda, reaching out to sweep the mess on to the floor. "I'm thinking!"

"Yes," said Yungstar, really peeved. "Thinking how your plan has failed! Just like all your plans fail!"

"Keep your evil tongue to yourself!" screamed Zelda. "You gluttonous wretch! I shall not be beaten by Terrahawks, do you hear?"

Yungstar cringed away, and his aunt Cystar's wig slipped over her eyes as he bumped into her. But suddenly, Zelda's attention was caught by something else, and she snatched for her crystal—the device that put her in touch with events on Earth! "Failed, have I? Not at all! Something is—*happening*!"

Though damaged, the Cube had put itself back in touch with its evil mistress, and Sam Oaky, peering at it, became hypnotised as the thing glowed and throbbed! Sam's eyes glazed over as Zelda's voice dinned into his brain. "You will obey! You will follow my instructions in every detail!"

Oaky sat down. "I will—obey," he intoned. "I am in your power!"

Out in the desert, Battlehawk lay at the foot of the rocks that rose sheer from the sand. From his perch, Sergeant Major Zero turned to Ninestein. "Sah. The Battletank's covered the whole area again. No sign of that Cube."

"There's not much more we can do, Tiger," put in Mary.

"No," agreed Ninestein. "Except—expect the unexpected."

At that moment, a message came through from Hiro on Spacehawk. The lieutenant had monitored a weak radio signal, and now he played back the cleaned-up recording of it. It was Zelda's hypnotic message to Sam Oaky, through the Cube.

"Can you give us the point of reception, Hiro?" said Ninestein.

"Yes, sir. Vaguely. It's certainly within twenty miles of your present location."

Ninestein turned to Mary and Zero. "It would be better if we moved around a little less conspicuously, Terrahawks being a secret organisation. Incognito, so to speak . . . "

"In *what*, sah?" said Zero.

"Incognito, Sergeant Major," said Ninestein irritably.

They left Battlehawk in Hudson, the computerised Rolls-Royce. Ninestein ignored Zero's joke that there weren't incognito, but in-car, and they set off for the main highway. Perhaps someone in the region had *found* that Cube.

They did not see Sam Oaky's cabin, well off the beaten track. The cabin in which, following Zelda's commands he was busy with tools, wood, and paint . . .

Sheriff Cy Bull sat up straight in his chair. Over the radio, on the desk, shrilled the excited voice of Deputy Sheriff Kilroy. "You ain't gonna believe this, Cy! I'm in pursuit of a grey Rolls-Royce! Must be doin' about a hundred miles an hour!"

"Then book it, Kilroy," spluttered Bull. "Give it the flashing lights an' the sirens!"

Zero said: "I think we've got company, sah."

"Shall I endeavour to lose this particular arm of the law?" put in Hudson.

"Why don't you do that," nodded Ninestein.

Additionally, as the speed increased, Hudson decided to alter his appearance, and the Rolls changed its colour from grey to red. "To match," said Ninestein, with a wry glance at Zero, "the fire in my eyes."

Patrolwoman Billie Jean Hollins saw it streak past. She called her boss. "Sheriff? You know that grey Royces-Rolls you told me to watch out for? The one Kilroy lost? Well, you should've said, Rollses-Royce."

"Never mind that," bawled Bull, over the radio. "Kilroy said it had speeded up to a hundred and thirty! Have you got it?"

"Not exactly. But a *red* Rollses-Royce has just gone past, doing a hundred and *sixty*!"

Bull sank back into his chair. "I don't believe it! Suddenly, my county is infested with Royces-Rolls in all the colours of the rainbow!" He did a horrified double-take as a screech of brakes made him look out of the window. For there, pulling up, was a *blue* Rolls-Royce (Hudson rather *liked* changing colour to avoid police cars) with two people and a shiny ball in it!

Bull could only gape as Ninestein burst in, with the briefest of introductions. The sheriff accepted Tiger's credentials, and said that, yes, something unusual had been found. Out at a place called Oaky's Corral . . . The Rolls pulled away again, and the sheriff began to beat his head on his desk. He could have sworn that the car had turned *green* . . .

Hudson pulled up beyond Sam Oaky's shack. And even as Ninestein got out, he heard the voice of Zelda, as if coming from nowhere. "I am delighted to see you," she said smoothly. "I have decided that there will be a duel. A duel to the death. One against one. *You*, against my Cube!"

"A gunfight at Oaky's Corral?" said Ninestein. He walked back to Hudson and picked up a laser-pistol. "Why not?"

"Tiger! It's suicide! You're no match for a Cube!" Mary looked aghast.

"Cool it, Mary," said Ninestein. "When it starts—get Sam Oaky out of that cabin. And you, Sergeant Major—well, you know what your task is."

"Yes, sah," said Zero. "Mustn't let that fire in your eyes burn out, must I?"

Tiger Ninestein knew that Zelda would play a dirty game. One against one? That wasn't her style. He ran for some rocks and, as the Cube leaped into view beyond him, fired at it. It disintegrated in a burst of splinters.

"So *that's* it! You've had Oaky make phoney Cubes, Zelda!"

Another appeared, to his left. Ninestein fired, and it blew apart.

"Yahh-haaa-haaa-*harrrgh*!" Zelda's voice cackled in triumph. "I *do* tell wicked lies, don't I? Be careful! To your right!"

Two Cubes sprang up. One false? One real? Ninestein swung the gun, and both fell. *Both* false. He was sweating now and, as he ran, he fell sprawling over a tripwire that Oaky must have laid down on Zelda's command. A Cube zipped down another wire towards him—but yet again it was a model! Ninestein lay prone, looking around feverishly.

"Are you enjoying our little confrontation?" screeched Zelda.

Another Cube appeared beyond him, and some instinct told Tiger Ninestein that, at last, this was the real thing. Desperately, he aimed, and squeezed the trigger. Nothing!

Another shriek of laughter from Zelda. "Fool! *Fool!* You need to re-charge! You should learn to *count*!"

The Cube played with him. It hovered there, and shots from it blew fragments of rock around his feet. "Get it over with, Zelda," yelled Ninestein. "But remember, there'll be another clone to replace me!"

"Allow me," cackled Zelda, "to enjoy the moment of your death. And rest assured, clone, one day you will be the last of your line! There is a *limit* to your powers of regenerating yourself!"

Ninestein knew it was true. He *was* a clone. But the process could *not* go on for ever. Like the proverbial cat, he only had so many lives. Nine lives? Ninestein lives? Crazy thoughts whirled in his head as he tensed himself for the inevitable blast of killing fire from the Cube.

And then the Cube exploded. Gloriously. Into spraying fragments. Gasping, Ninestein turned slowly, to see Sergeant Major Zero perched within the arms of a prickly cactus, having fired the shot that had destroyed the enemy and stilled Zelda's gloating voice.

"You took your time, Zero," croaked Ninestein.

"Well, it *is* rather prickly up here, sah," said Zero. He added: "Fair puts even the best military marksman off his aim, sah."

Ninestein relaxed. In pieces. First his neck, then his arms, then his legs. "How's Oaky?" he breathed.

"He's—er—Okay, if you'll pardon what sounds like a pun," said Mary, running over. "Dazed. Doesn't know what's happened."

Ninestein was gracious enough to help Zero down from the cactus. "The word, sah, is 'thanks'," said the Zeroid. "When we get home—perhaps—a medal . . . ?"

Hudson took them from the scene. And Sheriff Cy Bull, who was still trying to work out exactly who Tiger Ninestein was, got a call in his office. It was Patrolwoman Billie Jean Hollins. Reporting a *purple* Rollses-Royce that had just overtaken her.

Deputy Sheriff Kilroy broke in over the radio. "The heck with that," he said. "*I've* just seen an orange Royce-Rollses . . . "

Sheriff Cy Bull threw the set out of the window, put on his hat, and went on holiday . . .

THUNDER PATH

On the Martian base, Zelda's sister, Cystar, and Zelda's son, Yungstar, glanced nervously at the horrifying monster standing in front of Zelda herself. The beast was the Lord Sram, ready as always to do the evil queen's bidding.

Cystar said: "Using her genius to control matter, Zelda is about to transport you to Earth! Isn't that wonderful?"

"Don't ask him questions, imbecile," snapped Zelda to her sister. "You know what happens when he speaks!" Then Zelda turned and went into a kind of trance, sweat breaking out on her ugly brow. For long moments she concentrated all her powers—and, suddenly, Sram vanished! Instantly, he reappeared—but not on Mars. He stood, snorting softly, somewhere in the open wastes of a South American desert . . .

Many miles away, in Hawknest, Mary Falconer stood looking at Kate Kestrel in the Terrahawk Lounge. Kate was wearing a beautiful casual outfit in primrose, with a matching wig. She checked her appearance in a mirror. "You don't think the blue would be better . . . ?"

"Kate, you look perfect," said Mary. "Just right for a top recording star."

Kate frowned. "Unreliable, temperamental, bitchy. I wish I didn't have to pretend to be like that." But she knew that she was one of Terrahawks' contacts with the outside world, and had to play the part. Sighing, she made her way to Hawkwing's launch tunnel, and entered the Egg cockpit. Soon, Hawkwing was off and, at last, the wing section, with Hawkeye at the controls, separated from the main craft. "So long, Hawkeye," radioed Kate. "Parting is such sweet sorrow!"

"Never mind," laughed Hawkeye. "I'll see you on the morrow!"

Kate made for her own house—a fabulous home perched above some cliffs—a real pop-star's palace! The aircraft flew straight towards the cliff-face and seemed to disappear into it! Actually, it entered a docking bay invisible from the outside world.

Kate went to her room, tidied herself, and then came from the front porch to where Hudson, Tiger Ninestein's amazing Rolls-Royce, was waiting for her. Hudson, able to change his colour at will, matched the girl's outfit perfectly. "I hope you approve, madam," he said, and Kate chuckled.

"I certainly do. And now—to the studios. Fast. I'll be late, but that's how I'm supposed to act."

At the studios, the producer and his assistant welcomed Kate with oily smiles, treating her like the singing star she was. They would not have dared to complain that she had kept them waiting! And, like a queen, Kate swept into the recording room to begin running through a group of songs for her latest album . . .

Meanwhile, away in that remote South American desert, a giant land-train was speeding over rough country. This was the Overlander. A remotely controlled and programmed freighter which regularly brought supplies to Hawknest. As it approached him, the terrible monster, Sram, left the shelter of some rocks and stood facing it. He opened his mouth, exposing his fearsome teeth, and let loose a roar that made the earth tremble. The sound grew in volume until a huge landslide of rocks and boulders toppled from a nearby cliff-face, the whole mass collapsing to block the Overlander's path! The massive vehicle tried to surge up and over the barrier, but its giant wheels

slipped in the loose rubble, and it came to a shuddering halt. Sram's roar died away, and with no more than a grunt of satisfaction, he moved forward . . .

In Terrahawk Lounge, Tiger Ninestein turned from his video game as Mary Falconer said: "We have a problem. The Overlander has left its laser guidance path."

"Confound it," growled Ninestein irritably. "And just when I was in with a chance of beating my best score yet."

"Hullo! It's on the move again," exclaimed Mary. "What can be going on?"

"Do we have a fix, Sergeant Major?" said Ninestein, looking at his Zeroid commander, up on his perch.

"Yes, sah. The Overlander's at grid reference 0428. Heading due west."

"That's rugged country," put in Mary. "Even the Overlander can't cross that kind of terrain."

But Sram had smashed out the windscreen of the Overlander's driving unit and had taken over the controls. The train was heading fast towards a towering outcrop of rock—yet one mighty roar from Sram's astounding throat brought the whole mass of granite crashing in ruins, to clear a path for the Overlander to pass through without harm! There was no limit to the power of that terrible voice!

"It's *still* heading due west, sah," said Zero to Ninestein.

"I don't understand it," gasped Mary. "It appears to have driven clear through a mountain!"

Ninestein came to a decision. "I'm calling a ten-forty," he said.

The alarm sounded and, at once, Lieutenant Hawkeye left the lounge

and ran for Hawkwing's launch tunnel. And way out at the recording studios, Kate Kestrel was aware that a bangle she wore on her wrist was giving out a soft bleating, too quiet for anyone else to hear.

The producer was saying: "The run-through was great, Miss Kestrel. I'd like to go for a take straight away."

"Sorry, but I've got to leave," said Kate shortly, and left the recording men gaping at her in amazement.

The producer threw his papers on the ground and raved with fury as soon as the door had closed behind her. "I always knew she was temperamental, but *this* is ridiculous! One day, that woman's going to give me grey hairs!"

Kate didn't like acting in that way, but she could not ignore a ten-forty. She rejoined Hudson. "Actually, madam," he said, "it's a ten-fifty for you. You have to rejoin Hawkwing at once."

"Okay, Hudson," sighed Kate. "Go to it. And don't spare the horses. And when I'm gone, contact the recording studio, and make some excuses for me."

"But—but what am I to say, madam?" said Hudson, for once at a loss.

"Adopt your role as F. W. Runkin, my personal manager, Hudson. You'll think of something," grinned the girl.

Once at her home, Kate made for the Egg and, within moments, it was hurtling across the skies to rendezvous with the wing section of Hawkwing, Hawkeye at the controls. Dramatically, the two parts of the flying machine closed upon each other, turning together at the last moment to dock at full speed!

"We've got to stop meeting like this," said Hawkeye with a laugh. Then, more seriously, he added: "We have trouble with the Overlander, Kate."

In Terrahawk Lounge, Mary turned to Ninestein. "The Overlander's altered course again, Tiger."

"Hmm. I think we'd better get out there, too," he said. "Stand by for lift-off."

The Lounge, itself part of the massive transporter, Battlehawk, shuddered as the photon engines fired. The entire outside of the White House headquarters divided, and the huge craft began to rise into the air from the interior. Ninestein radioed Kate: "We're on our way. Report as soon as you have a sighting."

Her voice came back: "Ten-ten!"

Five minutes later, Kate was on again. "Visual contact! It's on heading 124. Speed, fifty knots."

Abruptly, Sergeant Major Zero began bouncing about on his perch beside Ninestein. "Sah! Sah! Listen . . . " He said excitedly.

"Shut up, Zero," snapped Ninestein. "I'm trying to think!"

"But, sah," insisted the Zeroid. "Heading 124! That means the Overlander is driving straight for Santa Verona!"

Ninestein gasped. "The *shale* refinery!" His mind pictured the vast complex of the Santa Verona oil-field. "There's a hundred million gallons of high octane aviation fuel in their storage-tanks!"

Grimly, Mary said: "I've checked the Overlander's cargo manifest. It's carrying forty-four percent explosive cargo!"

"Flaming thunderbolts!" exclaimed Ninestein. "We've got to stop it!"

"The Overlander's thirty miles from the refinery, sah," said Zero.

Kate, in Hawkwing, received her orders. "You can't destroy the Overlander, Kate. You'd be caught in the detonation. Try to divert it."

"Ten-ten," said Kate. She threw Hawkwing into a steep dive, and in the gun-bay, Hawkeye ranged his energy-cannons on a point ahead of the speeding land-train.

In the moment of attack, Sram lifted his fearsome face and roared violently through the broken windscreen. The bellowing force caught the diving aircraft and shook every rivet with its powerful vibrations!

"I—I can't hold her!" yelled Kate! "Fire, Hawkeye! *Fire!*"

Energy bolts lanced down and smashed craters in the Overlander's path—but the land-train merely swerved round the obstacles and resumed its course!

"I can't understand this," said Kate over the radio. "We were hit by some incredible sound-wave, Tiger. And, what's more, the way the Overlander changed course, I reckon there's a driver aboard!"

"A *driver*?"

Doctor Ninestein heard Mary Falconer's gasp, and bit his lip. "I have a theory," he said. "But I don't like what I'm coming up with!"

"Twenty-two miles from refinery," intoned Sergeant Major Zero.

Ninestein punched up a map of the area on his video display unit. "There might be one way to stop it," he said. "It has to cross the Verona bridge."

Battlehawk swung on to a new heading and, overflying the vast expanse of the refinery's shale-fields, it dropped Sergeant Major Zero and four of his Zeroids. Zero bounced once. He grunted: "Ooh. This

stuff's hard. As hard as Ninestein's heart!" But he knew his duty. To demolish the Verona bridge, spanning a vast chasm, at all costs.

"Right, lads," he confronted his Zeroids. "What we need is a length of pipe."

"Zat should not be too difficult to find," said the French-accented Zeroid 18. "Near a refinery for ze oil."

"In that case," barked Zero, "don't stand about jabbering! *Move!*" As Number 18 rolled off, Zero turned to Number 98, beside him. "Always stand downwind of 18, lad. They do say he puts garlic in his lubrication oil. Pheewwww!"

While Hawkwing continued to overfly, and Ninestein and Mary watched from Battlehawk, the Overlander drew closer and closer to the Verona bridge. "Just six miles," said Mary. "I hope Zero's going to make it in time!"

"He'd better," breathed Ninestein.

The Sergeant Major's Zeroids had set up the piping that Number 18 had uncovered. It was Zero's intention to use it as a kind of gun-barrel. "Now then, lads," he said. "You all know we can increase our mass."

"Sacre bleu!" said 18. "You mean we are going to fire ourselves out of zis?"

"Right, Dix-huit, mon ami," said Zero. "You never heard of human cannon-balls?"

"Oui! But I, numero Dix-huit, am no human!"

"Shut up and get in the pipe, lad," said Zero.

Next second, Number 18 was on his way. His wild war-cry—"Allez, allez, allez!" ended in a thundering crash as he landed among the bridge supports and smashed a whole section of them to fragments!

"Your turn now, 98," barked Zero.

Number 98 hit the target with as much force as 18—but still the bridge stood! And every moment, the Overlander drew nearer and nearer!

The other two Zeroids followed up, but at last it became clear to Zero that he'd have to make the trip himself. "Here I come," he shouted, hurling himself from the pipe. "*Geronimo!*"

It did the trick! Even as Zero's mass brought the bridge toppling down, the Overlander hung for a second in empty air and fell into the ravine! Shattered though it was, its cargo, mercifully, did not explode.

Ninestein whistled with relief. "Can you see the driver, Zero?"

Zero's voice was strained. "Oh, I can see him all right, sah. Not a pretty sight! A sort of—monster, sah. I really don't know how to describe him!"

"Well, what are you waiting for, Zero? *Try*, confound it!" snapped Ninestein.

"Huh. Too late, sah," said Zero. "You're not going to believe this, but he's gone. Vanished. Clean in front of me eyes!"

Ninestein turned to Mary. "As I thought," he said. "One of Zelda's."

"And, once more, she's reclaimed her own," said Mary, shivering.

There was nothing left to do but make arrangements for the recovery of the Overlander, the repair of the bridge, and the salvage of the cargo. It would keep them occupied for some time. "And the whole lot of 'em too busy to spare even a little 'thank-you' for me," grumbled Zero. "Bad-mannered lot, humans."

Kate was spared any part in the labour. It was several hours later that she returned to the recording studios to resume her session and make a great success of her album. "I had a call," said the producer, expertly concealing his bad temper from the star, "from your manager. Said you were—suddenly called away. Indisposed."

"That's right," smiled Kate. "It was nothing serious." She knew the man would simply put down another black mark against her so-called temperament but, privately, she smiled to herself. "If only you *really* knew," she thought . . .

MIND MONSTER

A transparent cylinder about six feet tall stood on the floor behind Zelda. The interior seemed to be filled with white, swirling mist. Yungstar had been asleep, but Zelda had ordered her sister, Cystar, to shake him awake. Now, irritable, grumbling, but as always in fear of Zelda, he faced his mother. "I have something to show you, my son," she said. "Look into this cylinder, and you will see something so terrible, so frightening, that it will numb your senses!"

Yungstar muttered, but did as he was told. Suddenly, he gave a yelp of dismay for, in the swirling mist, he saw the figure of Zelda herself—flames flaring around her head and body! She looked even more terrible than usual!

"Nyugggh!" Yungstar backed away, terrified. "Wh-what does it mean, mother?" he stuttered. "I d-don't understand!"

Zelda chuckled. "Neither will the accursed Terrahawks," she said . . .

On Spacehawk, Hiro had company. Kate Kestrel, on the space-station for a refresher course, watched him as he tended his beloved house-plants. Both of them turned as Space Sergeant 101 made a report.

"We have a contact. Alien ship."

"Lock on to it," ordered Hiro.

The intruder was a large ship. One of Zelda's transporters, known as the Rhino. "It's come to a halt just out of range," said 101.

"What's it up to?" said Kate, puzzled. "Hey, look! It's turning back, now. Heading the way it came!"

Hiro was as baffled as Kate, but then, neither of them knew that the Rhino had paused, only to release a six-foot long cylinder of transparent material . . .

On Earth, Kate's record producer was trying to get in touch with her. To him, she was a chart-topping singer. He, naturally, had no idea of her secret role as Hawkwing's pilot. "I've put in a call to F. W. Runkin, her manager," his assistant Stew Dapples told him.

Now, F. W. Runkin didn't exist. It was only a name, used by the Terrahawks' fantastic Rolls-Royce, better known—to them—as Hudson. Hudson was heading for Hawknest with Sergeant Major Zero in it as the car-intercom started. "That's almost certainly Anderburr Records," said Hudson. "I'm running out of excuses for Miss Kestrel. Will you take it, Sergeant Major?"

"Be a pleasure," said the Zeroid. "Hullo?"

"I'd like to speak to F.W. Runkin," said the voice at the other end.

"He's—er—out on the road," said Zero with a soft chuckle. "This is O'Naught."

"Do you know where Miss Kestrel is? It's very urgent," continued the voice.

"She's floating about somewhere," said Zero. "Tell you what, I'll have Mr. Runkin call you as soon as he's available. Goodbye for now!" Zero chuckled again. "Did you like that, Hudson?" he said. "Called meself O'Naught. Zero. O'Naught. Get it? It was a joke."

"Very *nearly*, Sergeant Major," said Hudson smoothly.

Meanwhile, in Hawknest itself, Doctor Tiger Ninestein had been told by Hiro of the Rhino spacecraft's odd behaviour. And now there was something else. The cylinder had been detected and, acting on his own authority, Hiro had had it fetched in for examination.

"It's empty, except for a mist of some sort," said Hiro. "What are your orders, sir?"

"You'd better have Zeroids open it up, Hiro," replied Ninestein. "But be careful. Expect the unexpected."

Kate Kestrel had gone down to watch Space Sergeant 101 and one of his soldiers drill into the thing. As they broke through, the mist seemed to vanish, but in the smallest fraction of an instant, Kate was sure that she heard an ominous, deep-toned noise. And, shaking her head, she was just as sure that, for a fleeting instant, she had seen the horrible figure of Zelda flit past her!

"Did—did you see anything, 101?" she said nervously.

"No, ma'am. Did you?"

"I—I—perhaps I imagined it," said Kate. She left, to make preparations for her return to Hawknest in Treehawk.

Hawknest's garage, at the side of the White House, had a sign illuminated on the closed doors. It read: 'Keep out. Car Wash in operation'. From inside, there came the sound of Hudson singing—just as a human might sing in the bath! An intercom buzzed in an anteroom, and Zeroid 18, on duty, answered it as Hudson's song ended, and he shouted: "Will someone answer that for me?"

It was the recording studio again. "I'm sorry," said the French-accented Zeroid. "Monsieur F. W. Runkin, 'e is taking ze bath. I am Dix-huit."

At Anderburr Records, Stew Dapples turned to his boss. "I'm talking to Des Wheat, sir. It's a terrible line."

"Well, tell him we need Miss Kestrel's last track for her latest album, and tell him we need it yesterday," raved the producer.

Zeroid 18 took the message. "Oui. I will tell Monsieur Runkin as soon as his body has been dried and polished."

"Polished?" The producer's assistant put down the phone and spread his hands. "Runkin has his body *polished*! What is he? Some kind of *nut*?"

Kate herself had arrived at Hawknest. She said hullo, briefly, to Mary, before she went to her quarters. But Mary Falconer remained standing like a statue, a frown on her face. There was a deep-toned noise. Somehow menacing. And it was inside her head. All at once, there was a terrifying roar, and there in the lounge, facing her, stood Sram—the fearsome monster with the power to destroy mountains with a single bellow of his mighty voice!

Mary screamed, but her scream was drowned as Sram opened his horrible throat and roared again! The walls shook, split and crumbled! The ceiling came down! The entire White House fell about Mary's ears, completely burying her—as if in a tomb!

Very slowly, she recovered her senses. She opened her eyes, and there were only Hawkeye and Ninestein, bending over her. There was nothing wrong with either the walls or the ceiling. Everything was in its proper place. "But—but he was *here*!" she gasped. "He—he roared . . . and everything collapsed!"

"Who, Mary, *who*? And what are you talking about?" Ninestein shook her, but not roughly. "You passed out—but *why*?"

Mary tried to explain, but she had to admit that it didn't make sense.

"Sram?" said Hawkeye. "Here? That's crazy! You can't believe it, Tiger!"

"I can't afford not to, Hawkeye," said Ninestein. "I want a top security search of this entire base. Immediately."

Hawkeye himself was the next victim of Zelda's strange and mysterious attack. In one of the corridors, he came face to face with Hiro, of all people. A Hiro strangely pale of face, and wearing a samurai headband round his brow. "What in thunder are you doing here?" said Hawkeye. "Wait—you're not Hiro at *all*!"

"No. I am Moid. The Master of Infinite Disguise," said the figure. "And my mission is to kill you!" He leapt at Hawkeye even as the lieutenant drew his gun, and, next moment, Moid was gripping Hawkeye's wrist, forcing him to turn the weapon on his own head!

Hearing the commotion, Sergeant Major Zero burst into the corridor.

"Sah!" he radioed to Ninestein. "Lieutenant Hawkeye seems to be fighting himself! He's about to blow his own brains out!"

"Stop him, Zero!" yelled Ninestein. "Use stun!"

The Sergeant Major extended his gun-probe, and a bolt of stunning force hit Hawkeye, who collapsed, unconscious, before he could kill himself. "Everyone around here's going barmy," said Zero, mystified. "Except me, of course."

On Mars, Zelda was rubbing her hands with glee. Her all-seeing crystal told her that her plan was succeeding. "The force is loose in the Terrahawks' lair," she cackled. "It will conjure up in their minds all the worst horrors they can imagine! They will destroy themselves!" She turned to Yungstar. "When you looked into the cylinder, you were frightened, my imbecile son! What was it you saw?"

"It—it was you, mother," said Yungstar nervously. But Zelda wasn't offended. She was delighted!

At Hawknest, Hawkeye had been brought round. "It *was* Moid," he told Ninestein. "I didn't *imagine* anything!"

"But Zero saw nothing," said Ninestein. "Maybe we're up against

something a human can experience, but a machine can't."

"Sah," protested Zero. "What's a human got that a Zeroid hasn't?"

"A complex imagination," snapped Ninestein.

Kate was with them. "I hear it again," she faltered. "The noise! Coming closer!" She darted to a doorway, and fancied she saw, for a moment, the figure of Zelda there in the darkness beyond. Kate fired her gun, but the image vanished. "It was Zelda—and she's down there somewhere," she said, and there was perspiration on her brow.

"We're up against some kind of mind force capable of inducing frightening hallucinations," said Ninestein grimly. "I have a theory about this, and I'm going on alone."

Kate recoiled. "You can't, Tiger. It's getting stronger. It could take over your mind completely!"

Yet there was no alternative. Numbly, Mary nodded for Zero to switch on the machine and, as they watched, they saw his body twist and turn on its couch.

Inside Ninestein's mind, even though he was now unconscious, it was as though a battle raged. He dreamed himself fighting Zelda, Sram, Moid, the Sporilla—all of them at once. Surely, they would destroy him!

But then, suddenly, he lay quiet.

"It's over," said Zero quietly. "Unhook him, lads."

"That's what I'm counting on, Kate," said Ninestein. He turned to Sergeant Major Zero. "You know what to do if it does?"

"Yes, sah," said the Sergeant Major.

Alone now, Tiger Ninestein made his way down the dark corridor. Now *he* heard the deep-toned noise. And all at once, the awesome form of another of Zelda's monsters—a Sporilla—emerged from the shadows! Screaming with hate, the Sporilla tore a chunk of masonry from the wall and hurled it at Ninestein, and he only just had time to duck before it crashed to splinters behind him.

"Stand by, lads," said Zero, turning to the four Zeroids who had come up at his command, carrying a stretcher. "Wait for my orders."

Now, down the corridor, Ninestein staggered about helplessly. To one side of him, Zelda appeared, cackling with triumph. To the other, Sram himself came into view, mouth open and ready to bellow. Beyond Sram, Moid loomed up, still disguised as Hiro. Ninestein screamed —even as Sram's arms seemed to close around his body . . .

"I'm going in," yelled Kate, unable to stand it any longer.

But Zero and his men beat her to it, and scooped the half-conscious figure of Ninestein on to the stretcher. "Leave it to me, ma'am," said Zero. "Doctor Ninestein's orders were to get him to the data dump. It's all set up."

The data dump was where the complex machinery lay that could duplicate Ninestein as a new clone, should he die. But now there was another machine made ready. One which could drain his brain, his mind, of all its contents! Mary Falconer joined Kate in time to see Ninestein coupled to this machine by Zero and his Zeroids.

"It's a terrible risk, Kate," whispered Mary.

"Yeah. But it was his idea, his theory," answered Kate, "to trap all the horrors of the alien force in his own mind, then filter them out."

"But if it doesn't work," said Mary, "we could wipe his brain clean permanently. It would even affect re-cloning!"

Mary ran to Ninestein's side and stroked his forehead. "Tiger! Can you hear me . . . ?" There was no response, and she looked round at Kate, her face a mask of horror.

"He don't look too bright," commented Sergeant Major Zero. "Maybe his mind *has* been wiped clean." He added: "What a terrible pity that would be!"

"I'm sorry to disappoint you, Zero." Ninestein sat up, blinking his eyes.

"Tiger!" Mary's eyes were full of tears. Tears of relief.

"I do believe you were worried about me, Mary," said Ninestein.

"Tiger!" said Mary again. "What you did was a marvellous, brave . . . " (here, her voice changed in tone) " . . . foolhardy, pig-headed, stupid, *crazy* thing to do!"

Ninestein grinned at her. "Nice to be loved," he said.

Later, a container which had been clipped to the mind-scanner, and which now contained the power-force that Zelda had sent, was mounted on top of a small space-rocket. It was fired from Treehawk's launch tunnel, and exploded harmlessly, far out in space, where it could do no further damage.

Once again, Zelda's plans had been foiled, and the Terrahawks could relax. Well, most of them, at any rate.

Hudson, unhappily for him, had been taking more desperate calls from Kate Kestrel's agonised record-producer, and Kate herself was wondering how on earth she could record the last track of her album in time.

"Record it from here," suggested Ninestein. "We can relay the track via Spacehawk directly into Anderburr Records' recording equipment. A simple enough matter, for us.

"But, Tiger," protested Kate. "The producer won't understand how it's done! He'll think I'm some kind of super-being!"

"So, he can keep guessing for the rest of his life, Kate," smiled Ninestein. "And besides, you *are* a super-being, as far as I'm concerned!"

The others agreed with him, as they listened to Kate cut her disc!

TO CATCH A TIGER

The small cargo spaceship, battered and grimy, was on its way back to Earth. It was the space equivalent of a 'tramp steamer', and the two men inside, Davis and Cole, were a scruffy pair who had decided to make a little detour. They were close enough to Mars, and knew that Mars had been placed 'off limits' by the World Government. But they didn't know *why*.

"There's something worth having there, Cole," said Davis. "Gold, maybe. Diamonds? Why don't we see if we can get our hands on some?"

"Okay," said Cole. "Nothing venture, nothing gain. We'll switch to manual control."

They little knew that Mars was off limits purely because the planet was now Zelda's base! Alert as always, the evil, witch-like queen saw the ship's approach.

"Two earthlings lurk in the interior," she said, while her son, Yungstar, hovered beside her, and her sister, Cystar, looked on nervously. "It is a transporter."

"What is the cargo, mother?" said Yungstar, and began to dribble hungrily as she replied: "Some kind of mineral ore. What does it matter? Launch the Zeaf and destroy the earth scum!"

"It might be something mouth-wateringly delicious," said Yungstar. "Crunchy galena—or copper pyrites! Damage it and bring it down intact, mother!"

At first, Zelda was about to rage at her son, but then she paused. "I shall bring it down," she said. "But not to satisfy your disgusting appetite, Yungstar. Perhaps I can use the two earthlings as—hostages!"

The Zeaf, Zelda's fighter, sped upwards from Mars and intercepted the cargo ship. A single shot was enough to knock out the craft's control area, and while Cole and Davis sat terrified, unable to understand what was going on, they were brought down to a soft landing not far from Zelda's base. It was not much later that Yungstar brought them, as captives, into Zelda's presence.

"Listen to me, earthlings," said Zelda to the horrified men. "You are at my mercy. Any attempt to escape will be foolish. You are bait, do you hear? Bait! To catch a Tiger!" She cackled with laughter as Cole and Davis looked at each other, terrified. Not knowing what she was talking about. She cackled again as Yungstar hustled them off to a cell.

The Tiger in question, Doctor 'Tiger' Ninestein, no less, soon learned what it was all about. Zelda had demanded an exchange. The lives of her two prisoners in return for his, and at once he had agreed. He turned to Sergeant Major Zero, in the Terrahawk Lounge. "Is the briefing set up?"

"Yes, sah," said Zero. And Ninestein went through to explain the plan he had devised to Mary Falconer, Kate Kestrel, Hawkeye and Sergeant Major Zero himself. They listened attentively and, at last, Ninestein said: "So that's it. Any questions?"

There were none. "Okay," said Ninestein. "We can work out the final details on the way to Mars."

"I hate being left out of this, Tiger," said Kate unhappily.

He shook his head. "You're far from left out, Kate. You are vital to the whole operation. I may be a clone, with nine lives, but I'm not going to give Zelda the satisfaction of killing me if I can help it. And you, staying here on Earth, are my most important link."

"Well—the best of luck, Tiger," said Kate. "It's going to rely on timing. I sure hope there are no snags."

Treehawk lifted off for Spacehawk, and soon, Ninestein, Mary, Hawkeye and Zero were being welcomed aboard the huge craft by Lieutenant Hiro. There was a great deal to do as Spacehawk moved out of orbit and, photon-drive blasting, began its journey across the Solar System towards Mars . . .

Meanwhile, Kate Kestrel, in one of her superb casual outfits, had joined her personal Zeroid, 55, in Ninestein's computerised Rolls-Royce, Hudson. Hudson had, gentlemanly car that he was, changed his colour to match Kate's clothes.

"Timing's the thing on this one, Hudson," said Kate. "We have to allow for transmission time to Mars. There's a lot of calculation involved."

"I understand that, madam," said Hudson.

Zeroid 55 chipped in. "Leave it to me. I'm pretty quick—at arithmetic."

Kate laughed. "Right. Well, on this mission, we're all three a team."

"Thank you, madam," said Hudson, pleased. "I, for one, will do my absolute utmost."

"If utmost is where it's at—I'm your cat!" said 55.

"Check," said Kate. "*Go*, Hudson. Anderburr Records, the recording studios . . . "

On Spacehawk, Hawkeye reported to Ninestein. "The landing capsule is ready, sir," he said. "And modifications are under way on this craft itself."

"We'll need a call-sign for the landing capsule," said Ninestein.

"How about M.E.V.?" suggested Hawkeye. "Martian Exploration Vehicle."

"Ten-ten," said Ninestein. "M.E.V. it is."

Spacehawk went into parking orbit well above Mars. Hiro and his Zeroid crew were on full alert, in case of trickery from Zelda, but there was no attack and, at last, the M.E.V. left the big ship for the surface. Mary Falconer had never felt so worried as now, as she watched it go. "Tiger, be careful down there," she whispered.

"Ninestein is on his way," said Zelda, watching the M.E.V.'s approach on her crystal.

"Is he alone, Zelda?" said Cystar.

"There's a metallic sphere with him," replied Zelda. "But the foolish clone is almost within my grasp! Tell Yungstar to bring the prisoners here!" She turned, and spoke to a figure standing nearby. It was Moid—the Master of Infinite Disguise. But this time he resembled nobody. He was just a sinister shape with a completely blank face. He was in his role as her executioner—her chief torturer! "You will see that he dies slowly, Moid," said Zelda. "With much, much pain!"

"You may be sure of it, Zelda," said Moid. "I shall go and prepare the Killing Chamber . . . "

Alone now, Zelda got ready for her personal moment of triumph. "So, clone," she rasped, as Ninestein entered, "we meet again—but this time, in my domain!"

"Let the hostages go, Zelda," said Ninestein calmly. He glanced across as Yungstar led in the trembling Cole and Davis. "Take them back to Spacehawk, Zero," said Ninestein.

Sergeant Major Zero, beside him, said: "I'll tell you straight, sah, I don't trust any of 'em. Permission to stay, sah!"

"Refused," said Ninestein.

Zelda shook a shrivelled hand impatiently. "Do as your master says, you spherical nonentity! It is the last order he will ever give you."

Reluctantly, Zero led the men out to the M.E.V. and, shortly, it took off for Spacehawk. The two men were too numb and shaken to wonder what was going on, and they were put in safe charge as Spacehawk began to move away from Mars. On the control deck, Hawkeye turned to Hiro. "Modifications complete?"

"Perfectry," said Hiro, muffing his 'L' as usual. "Once we are out of contact, I will activate the special shield which will make us invisible from Mars. And then we can return, unseen."

"It does mean we can't make direct contact with Tiger," said Mary nervously.

"Sure, Mary," soothed Hawkeye. "But that's where *Kate* comes in. And we have to make certain *she* gets her timing right . . . "

On Mars, Yungstar turned to his aunt and his mother. "They have gone," he said. "They have deserted their Ninestein."

"How will Moid carry out the execution?" said Cystar.

"For his pleasure, and my entertainment," chuckled Zelda. "After a long session in the Killing Chamber, I shall dissect the clone and see what makes him tick!"

"Expecting me to beg for mercy, Zelda?" asked Ninestein evenly.

"No, clone," chuckled Zelda. "Expecting you to *die*!"

Meanwhile, Kate Kestrel, as a chart-topping internationally successful singer, had astonished her long-suffering producer by arriving at the studios unannounced. Playing her part as a temperamental super-star, she had demanded a fully networked, live broadcast at once, and she'd got it. People fell over themselves doing her bidding. She was, secretly, a little worried about the song she was going to sing. She was ready, with her micro-communicator, to receive instructions from Spacehawk, and she would have to make sure that those instructions were coded into her song. They would be meaningless to her public, but they would be of vital importance to Tiger Ninestein. She just hoped she could work it all out in time . . .

Knowing that all this would be going on, Tiger Ninestein looked more confident than he felt. His nerves were getting strained as Zelda got more and more impatient. "What's holding up Moid?" she raved. "Hasn't he got the Killing Chamber ready *yet* . . . ?"

Spacehawk, its 'invisibility' electronic shield at full power, had returned to its post above Mars. Space Sergeant 101 reported: "Two minutes, fourteen seconds ahead of battle schedule."

"I'll contact Kate," said Mary. "Two minutes, fourteen seconds? She'll have to code it into her song, so that Tiger understands."

At the same time, in the M.E.V., which had also been modified to include an 'invisibility' shield, Hawkeye took off back to the Martian surface and, moments later, Sergeant Major Zero and some of his Zeroid soldiers launched themselves in the landing-craft's wake, too small in themselves to be picked up by Zelda's scanners.

Tiger Ninestein sat impassively in Zelda's headquarters. On his lap reposed the briefcase he'd brought with him. It contained a small video display unit, but Zelda hadn't bothered to take it away from him. Gloating, she said: "The Killing Chamber is almost ready, clone! Why do you not show fear?"

He shrugged. "Wouldn't give you that satisfaction."

"You *will* be afraid," she promised. "Soon, your screams will echo through this entire place!" She turned to Yungstar. "Let us *show* him the chamber, my son!"

From Anderburr's recording studio on Earth, Kate Kestrel began to sing her song. With Zeroid 55's aid, she had modified the lyric, and now her voice rang out, to the delight of all who listened. All over the country, people would be tuned in, to listen and enjoy, but to Kate, only one person mattered as an audience, and that was Tiger Ninestein!

He heard her, too. Flipping open his case so that the song came through, loud and clear. *And* he understood. "Two minutes, fourteen seconds ahead of schedule," he said to himself, even as Zelda moved towards him.

She tore the case from his hands, but the case didn't matter any more. One half of Ninestein's mind ticked off the seconds of a countdown while the other half argued with Zelda—kept her from thrusting him towards Moid's infernal device in the Killing Chamber.

"Six—five—four—three—two—ONE!"

Ninestein leapt into action! He snatched Zelda's stick from her hands and smashed her crystal with it. She screamed in fury as, at the same moment, Sergeant Major Zero and his Zeroids attacked the Martian base!

Zelda's Cubes—her own equivalent of Zeroids—put up a stiff resistance. But the surprise was too much! "Come on, lads! For the honour of the good old regiment!" yelled Zero, driving the enemy before him. "One more charge, and we're in!"

Yungstar and Cystar, in a frenzy of panic, raced this way and that, and Zelda was screaming at Moid. "Kill the clone! Kill him now! *At once!*"

Too late! For with a shattering crash, the wall of the room burst inwards as Sergeant Major Zero, having increased his mass, used himself like an unstoppable battering-ram!

More Zeroids burst through. Zelda was sent sprawling. Even Moid was bowled over by the rush, and now smoke-bombs were let off to make the confusion complete!

"This way, sah!" rasped Zero. "Follow me!" Ninestein was out through the jagged hole in a flash, and the Sergeant Major sounded the retreat. All of them—there had been not a single casualty—made for Hawkeye's M.E.V.—and though there were Cubes that tried to wing them, the rescue party were clear within seconds, and back on their way to Spacehawk!

"I *curse* the Terrahawks!" raved Zelda, in the ruins of her Killing Chamber. "Shall I *never* be able to overcome their infernal powers . . .?"

Yungstar and Cystar had made the best of the smoke to sneak away and hide. It would be a long time before Zelda's fury cooled off, and they were quite willing to let Moid take the brunt of her anger in the meantime . . .

In fact, Spacehawk was back in Earth orbit itself before Zelda had stopped shrieking. Not that Ninestein and his companions knew anything about *that*. They were all thinking of having a rather nice celebration party down in the White House.

"We'll get Kate to sing for us," said Ninestein.

"Now, now, Tiger," smiled Mary. "After today, I think it's *our* turn to sing for *her*, don't you?"

"Whatever's she done to deserve *that*?" chuckled Sergeant Major Zero . . .

21
18